LET'S FIND OUT! WEATHER

WHAT IS WEATHER FORECASTING?

LYNNAE D. STEINBERG

Britannica Educational Publishing
IN ASSOCIATION WITH
ROSEN
EDUCATIONAL SERVICES

For my family and friends, who support everything I try and tell me I can do it

Published in 2015 by Britannica Educational Publishing (a trademark of Encyclopædia Britannica, Inc.) in association with The Rosen Publishing Group, Inc.
29 East 21st Street, New York, NY 10010

Distributed exclusively by Rosen Publishing.
To see additional Britannica Educational Publishing titles, go to rosenpublishing.com.

First Edition

Britannica Educational Publishing
J. E. Luebering: Director, Core Reference Group
Mary Rose McCudden: Editor, Britannica Student Encyclopedia

Rosen Publishing
Hope Lourie Killcoyne: Executive Editor
Jacob R. Steinberg: Editor
Nelson Sá: Art Director
Nicole Russo: Designer
Cindy Reiman: Photography Manager

Library of Congress Cataloging-in-Publication Data

Steinberg, Lynnae D., 1957–
What is weather forecasting?/Lynnae D. Steinberg.—First edition.
pages cm—(Let's find out! Weather)
Includes bibliographical references and index.
Audience: 3–6.
ISBN 978-1-62275-795-4 (library bound) — ISBN 978-1-62275-796-1 (pbk.) —
ISBN 978-1-62275-797-8 (6-pack)
1. Weather forecasting—Juvenile literature. I. Title.
QC995.S795 2015
551.63—dc23

2014023246

Manufactured in the United States of America

Photo Credits:
Cover, p. 1 Harvepino/Shutterstock.com; p. 4 © AP Images; p. 5 Image Source/Getty Images; p. 6 Vladimir Mijailovic/Shutterstock.com; p. 7 NASA Earth Observatory; p. 9 stockshoppe/Shutterstock.com; p. 10 Vanessa Van Ryzin/Mindful Motion Photography/Moment/Getty Images; p. 11 Photos.com; p. 12 age fotostock/SuperStock; p. 13 Mark Burnett/Photo Researchers/Getty Images; p. 14 Pat Rafferty Productions; p. 15 Joe Raedle/Getty Images; p. 16 subtik/E+/Getty Images; p. 17 National Weather Service/NOAA; p. 18 Dorling Kindersley/Getty Images; p. 20 Photo Researchers/Science Source; p, 21 SSgt. Oscar M. Sanchez-Alvarez-USAF/U.S. Department of Defense; p. 22 Jay Directo/AFP/Getty Images; p. 23 Astronaut Ed Lu/Image courtesy of Mike Trenchard/Earth Sciences & Image Analysis Laboratory/Johnson Space Center/NASA; p. 24 Mike Coniglio/National Severe Storms Laboratory/NOAA; p. 25 David Epperson/Photodisc/Getty Images; p. 26 Scott Olson/Getty Images; p. 27 Maurice van der Velden/E+/Getty Images; p. 28 GSFC Scientific Visualization Studio/NASA; p. 29 Sepp Friedhuber/Vetta/Getty Images; interior pages background image solarseven/Shutterstock.com.

Contents

What Should I Wear Today?

The weather on Earth is always changing. Some patterns, like our seasons, are predictable. They come and go at the same times each year. Other patterns and events change often. Meteorology is a field of science that studies the changes in weather on a day-to-day basis in a specific place. Scientists who study meteorology are called meteorologists.

Here a meteorologist uses a special symbol on a map to show the path a storm might take. This helps warn people about the storm.

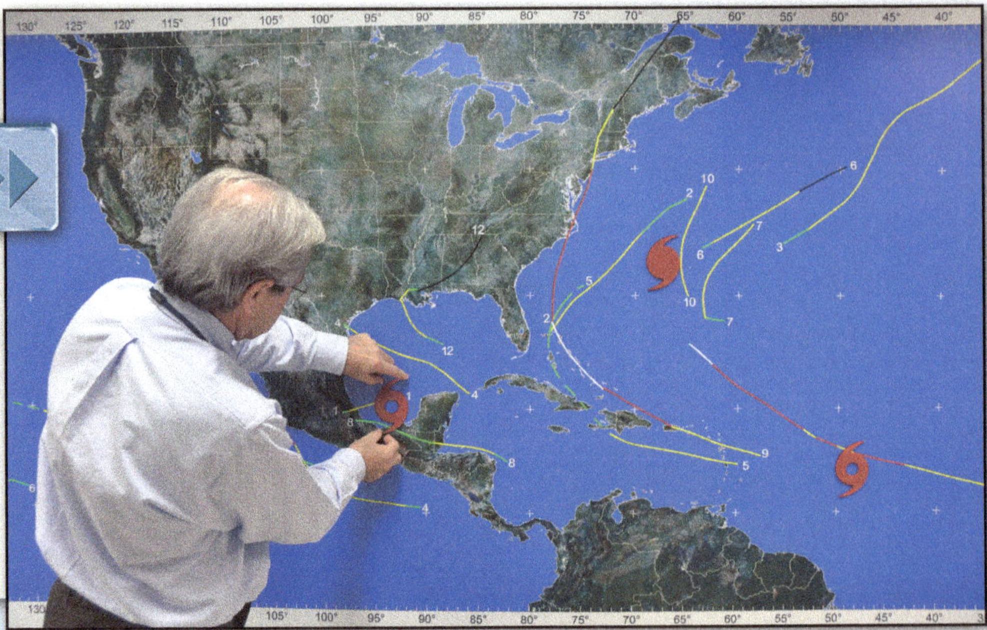

Using past history, patterns, and various measurement tools, meteorologists can tell whether it will rain or snow and whether it will be warm or cold. These scientists are able to tell people what the weather will be like anywhere in the world. This is called forecasting.

Climatology is the study of climate. Climate is the average weather conditions of a particular place or region over a period of years. Climatologists observe and study weather patterns on Earth over a long period of time.

Weather forecasters use maps to help people understand upcoming weather conditions for the days and weeks ahead.

Compare and Contrast

In what ways are weather and climate different? How are they the same?

What Is Weather?

Weather is the daily state of the atmosphere in any given place. The atmosphere is made up of the gases that surround Earth. Weather takes place in the lowest level of the atmosphere.

To most of us, the weather means things like it is hot and sunny outside or it is cold and rainy. To a meteorologist, the weather is a combination of certain

Most of Earth's weather, including the wind and most clouds, exists in the lowest level of the atmosphere.

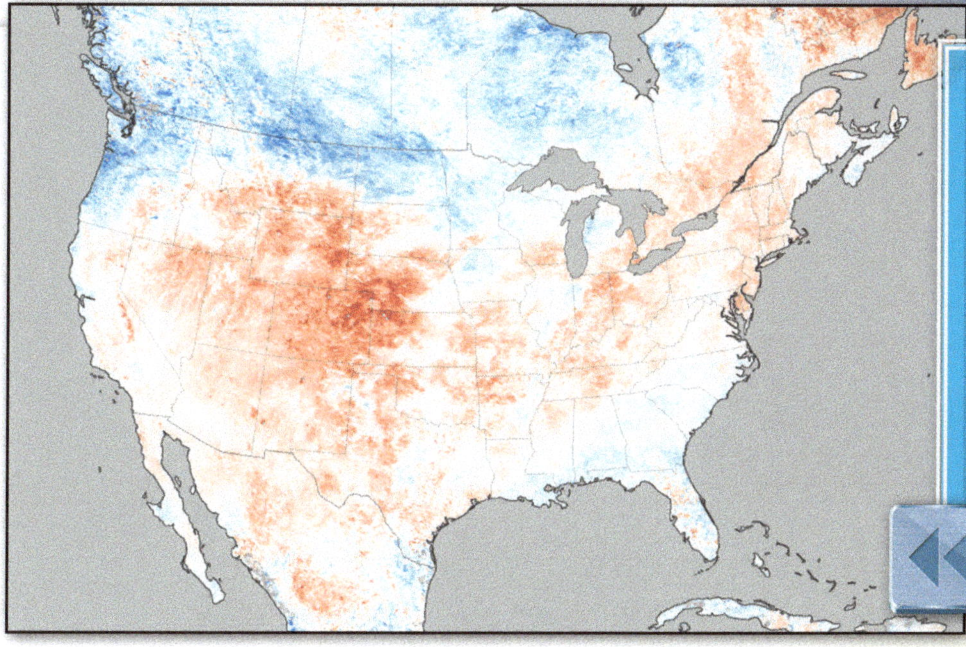

Colors are often used on weather maps to highlight areas of higher (red) or lower (blue) temperature ranges.

features. A meteorologist can watch and measure those features to tell what will happen with the weather. The main features that make up the weather are temperature, air pressure, wind speed and direction, humidity, and precipitation.

Temperature is a measurement of how hot or cold the air is. Energy from the Sun heats the air on Earth. But the energy from the Sun does not reach all parts of Earth equally or at the same time. So some areas are warmer than others.

Compare and Contrast

What is the weather like in places that get a lot of sunlight? How is it different in places that do not get a lot of sunlight?

The temperature of the air affects the air pressure and winds. The gases in the atmosphere have weight that presses down and creates atmospheric, or air, pressure. Warm air weighs less than colder air. As the Sun warms the air, the air spreads and moves upward. Colder air around it then moves in. The result is wind. Wind has a great effect on weather.

Water also plays an important part in the weather in several ways. When oceans, lakes, and other bodies of water on Earth heat up, some of the water evaporates into the air. The amount of moisture in the air is called humidity. Warm air can hold more moisture than cold air.

When water evaporates, it turns into a gas called water vapor and rises into the air.

When air cools, **water vapor** begins to turn back into a liquid. The water is in the form of

Water has been cycling since Earth formed. The water in your cup may have been sipped by dinosaurs!

tiny droplets. Many droplets together make clouds. Sometimes the droplets combine and form larger drops. If these drops get heavy enough, they fall to Earth as precipitation in the form of rain or snow.

Weather Forecasting in the Past

Long ago, before people knew about the science of weather, they tried to find ways to forecast the weather. It was important to know about the weather so they would know what crops to plant and when to plant them.

Some people believed that the gods controlled the weather. Other people looked into the sky and studied what they could see, such as the clouds. They looked for patterns so they could know what to expect. Others even studied the behavior of animals. They believed animals' behavior changed before storms or other changes in weather. They

Does your dog seem nervous or get under the bed before a storm? Animals sometimes sense changes in weather.

An **almanac** is a book containing a calendar and facts about the movements of the Sun, the Moon, and the planets. An almanac may also give weather predictions and other information of general interest.

recorded their observations in books called almanacs.

In ancient times, the famous Greek thinker Aristotle wrote about his own weather observations. His book on weather was important for more than 2,000 years. However, today we know that some of his information was incorrect.

People have been trying to understand the science of weather since the time of the Greek thinker Aristotle.

Learning the Science Behind Weather

In ancient times, people used their own observations to forecast the weather. Later people learned the science of the different weather features. They learned about such things as atmospheric pressure and humidity. They were able to create tools to study these features. These tools include the thermometer

Have you ever felt your ears pop on a plane? This is due to changes in air pressure, which we measure with a barometer.

Think About It

Why is it important to study weather information from many different places?

to measure temperature, the barometer to measure air pressure, and the hygrometer to measure humidity.

In the 1800s, the telegraph was invented. The telegraph was a system for sending messages over long distances quickly. It allowed scientists to collect and study weather information from many regions on Earth. Other new technology let meteorologists explore the upper atmosphere. They did this by attaching instruments to balloons, kites, and airplanes. These inventions helped meteorologists make more complete forecasts.

Weather balloons are still used today to gather information. They travel with the wind.

Forecasting Today

Today meteorologists have many tools to help them forecast the weather. In addition to the basic tools such as thermometers and barometers, they now have radar, satellites, and computers.

Radar is a system that uses waves of energy to sense objects. It can find a faraway object and tell how fast it is moving. Weather forecasters use it to locate storms and help predict the weather. Satellites are machines sent into outer space to travel around the planet. They take pictures

The same radar technology that can catch a car speeding down the highway is used to track the speed of weather fronts.

and send back information about the weather conditions happening all around Earth. Scientists take that information and study it. Computers help the scientists see patterns in the data that they gather.

Data is information that can be used in calculating, reasoning, or planning.

Today computer-drawn maps forecast wind, temperature, and humidity patterns for many levels of the atmosphere. Scientists use mathematical calculations to predict high and low temperatures, precipitation, winds, and other weather elements.

Meteorologists at the National Hurricane Center use computers to watch and track hurricanes.

WEATHER MAPS

Meteorologists create forecast maps to predict weather events. They use data collected from satellites and other measurement tools to create these maps. Symbols and colors are used on weather maps to show the conditions observed at weather stations. The weather observations used for these maps are collected at thousands of weather stations around the world four times a day. Meteorologists then use this information to predict how the weather will continue changing.

Information gathered from this meteorological center in Iceland will be shared with scientists around the world.

An important use of weather maps is to warn people about storms and other dangerous weather. Meteorologists use radar and satellite maps to follow the movement of dangerous weather features. This helps them warn people about approaching bad weather. One of the newest ways to predict danger from the weather are **storm surge** maps. These maps predict flooding in coastal areas.

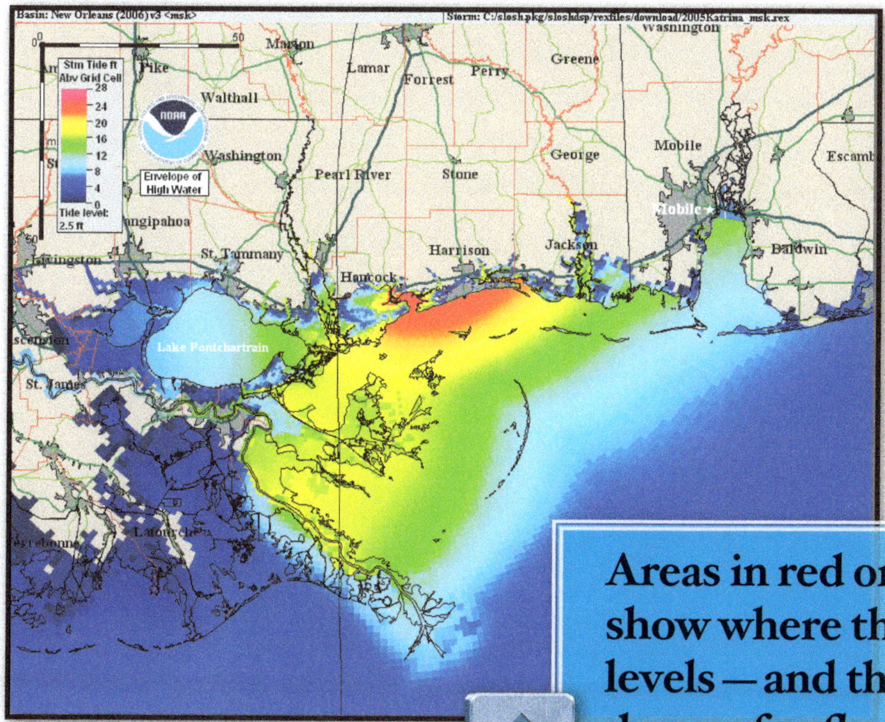

After some storms, there is a rise in sea level called a **storm surge**. This rise in the height of the sea causes flooding in areas along coasts.

Areas in red on a storm surge map show where the highest water levels—and therefore the greatest danger for flooding—may occur.

One common type of weather map shows the movement of weather fronts. A weather front is a sharp

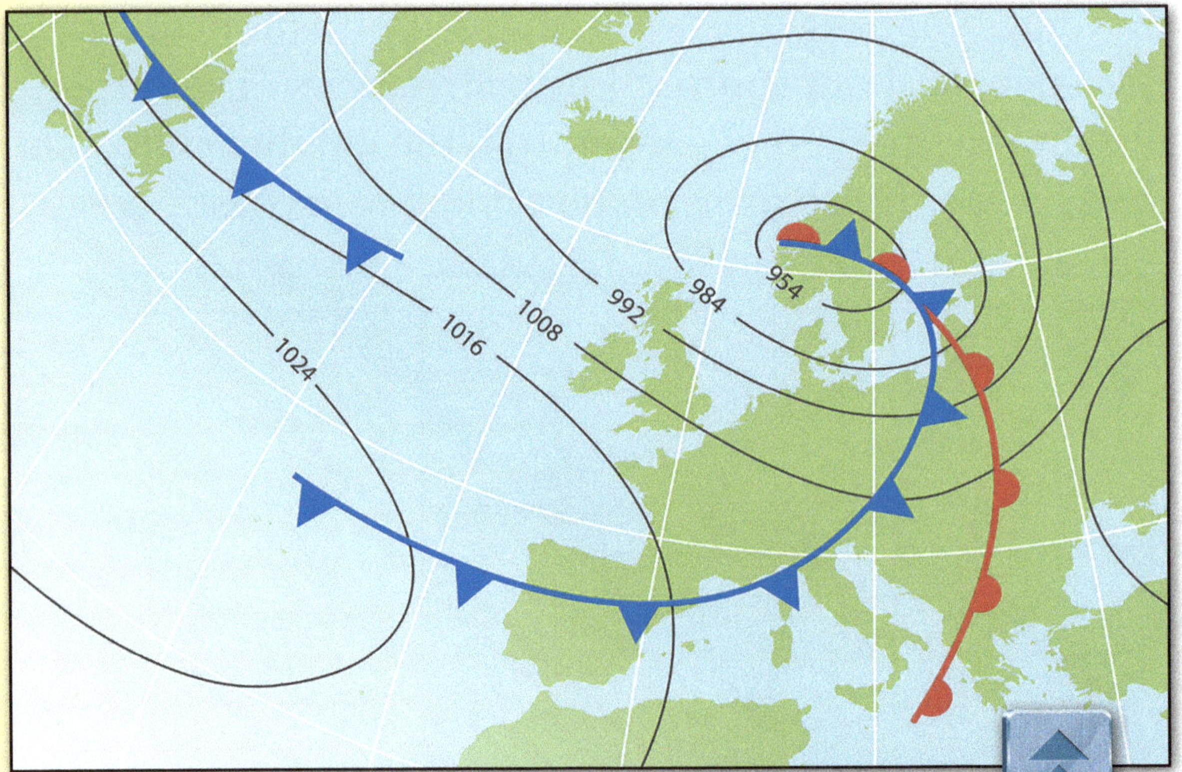

The swirls and curves you see on weather maps show the leading edges of air masses and in which direction they are moving.

boundary between two different air masses. Air masses are areas of similar types of weather. A cold front is the leading edge of a cold air mass. Cold fronts bring a quick drop in temperature and a fast rise in pressure. They are often accompanied by thunderstorms in summer and snow flurries in winter.

On a weather map, a cold front is shown as a blue line with triangles. The direction in which the triangles point is the direction in which the front is moving. A warm front is the boundary between a cold air mass that is retreating and a mass of warm air. On a weather map, a warm front appears as a red line with semicircles. The direction in which the semicircles point indicates where the front is moving.

Think About It

There is another type of front called a stationary front. A stationary front is the boundary where a warm front and a cold front meet and stop moving. Using both blue triangles and red semicircles, how do you think weather maps show stationary fronts?

FLOODS

One dangerous weather event that meteorologists predict using tools is flooding. Tools called rain gauges measure the amount of rainfall. Another tool called a hygrometer measures humidity, or moisture in the air. Most flooding is caused by heavy rains over a long period of time. Even if the rain is not happening where you live, you may be affected by it! The ground can become saturated (full of water). Then the rainwater has nowhere to go. That water can end up in a farmer's fields or in peoples' homes.

Flooding can be worse if there is not

One type of hygrometer uses both a dry-bulb and a wet-bulb thermometer to measure the relative humidity in the air.

Floodwaters can damage buildings and hurt people. The high waters of a flood may also carry disease and bacteria.

Think About It

Why do you think vegetation around a river can affect the amount of flooding?

much vegetation, or plants, on the land around rivers. Flash floods are the result of sudden heavy rainfall. They happen quickly and can be deadly.

Flash floods can catch people in fast-rising water before they have a chance to escape. A completely dry riverbed can fill up in just a few minutes! Accurate forecasting of floods can save lives.

Cyclone Watch!

Meteorologists can accurately predict when and where major types of storms will occur. This is important in keeping people safe from dangerous storms. One storm meteorologists track is called a cyclone. A cyclone is a system of winds that spiral. When such a storm forms over warm oceans close to the equator, it is called a tropical cyclone. Tropical cyclones are also called hurricanes or typhoons in different parts of the world. Their winds swirl at speeds higher than 74 miles (119 kilometers) per hour.

A meteorologist tracks the swirling motion of a cyclone on his computer to forecast where the storm will go.

Meteorologists know what conditions must be present for a cyclone to form. These conditions include certain wind patterns, air pressure measurements, and large ocean patterns such as El Niño. When meteorologists know these conditions, they can figure out when cyclones are likely to form. Once a cyclone has formed, it can be tracked using radar. This lets meteorologists warn people who live in the path of the storm to leave the area or take cover.

El Niño is the appearance every few years of unusually warm water in the eastern Pacific Ocean along the equator.

Tropical cyclones have cloudless centers known as eyes, which are calm. Once the eye has passed overhead, the opposite side of the storm hits.

Other Storms

Meteorologists can also predict tornadoes. A tornado is a type of storm in which powerful rotating winds form a column of air that reaches down toward the ground. When weather conditions are likely to result in a tornado, meteorologists announce a tornado watch. Tornado winds are the fastest on Earth. The winds in a tornado can reach speeds of nearly 300 miles (500 kilometers) per hour.

Tornadoes can be very destructive, and they form quickly. This is why it is important to know that one might be headed your way. In the United States, an agency called the National Weather Service operates a National Severe

Meteorologists have special trucks with equipment to study tornadoes in order to learn more about them and warn people.

Storms Forecasting Center in Missouri. Forecasters there watch the atmosphere for the conditions that can create tornadoes or severe thunderstorms.

Winter storms can be powerful as well. Storms featuring low temperatures, strong winds, and large amounts of snow are called snowstorms. The strongest are called blizzards. A blizzard has winds of more than 35 miles (56 kilometers) per hour for at least three hours.

Compare and Contrast

How are cyclones and tornadoes similar? How are they different?

When people are warned of upcoming blizzard conditions, they are better able to prepare.

Heat Waves and Cold Snaps

Waves are long periods of extreme heat or cold that affect a large area. In some regions, a cold wave is known as a cold snap or a cold spell. Studying the temperature and air pressure patterns allows scientists to forecast these extreme conditions. Although people may expect warm temperatures in the summer and cold temperatures in the winter, they may not be prepared for extreme temperatures.

Extreme heat can lead to **drought**.

A farmer looks at the damage that an extended drought caused to his once-green fields.

Drought can be dangerous to people and it can ruin crops. Unusually cold temperatures can be dangerous for people as well. If there is warning of a heat or cold wave, people can be prepared to deal with it. Power companies can prepare as well. They can plan for people to use more electricity to run heaters in the cold or air conditioners in the heat.

Drought is a long period without rain.

A greenhouse will help protect plants from an early snowfall by trapping warmer air inside and keeping freezing air out.

Climate Forecasting

Forecasting today has an important new use. Instead of just forecasting the weather for the next few days, scientists can now look at what the climate will be like over the next few decades. To study climate, scientists look at several conditions, including the greenhouse effect. The greenhouse effect is a warming of Earth's surface and the air above it. It is caused by gases in the air that trap energy from the Sun. Without the

Areas of rising temperatures can be seen in red on this map of Antarctica.

Too much heat being trapped in Earth's atmosphere is shrinking the habitats of several species on our planet.

Global warming is the trend of slow increases in the average temperature on Earth.

greenhouse effect, Earth would be too cold for life to exist.

Scientists believe that humans are increasing the greenhouse effect through their actions. When people drive a car, work in a factory, or use electricity at home, they burn coal, oil, and other fuels. Burning these fuels may add extra gases to the air. The extra gases trap more heat. Scientists think that this has led to global warming. Forecasters are working hard to predict how much of an effect global warming will have in the future on nature and Earth's resources.

Glossary

atmosphere The whole mass of air surrounding Earth.

atmospheric pressure The weight of the air; also known as barometric pressure.

barometer An instrument that measures the pressure of the atmosphere.

blizzard A powerful snowstorm caused by low temperatures, strong winds, and large amounts of snow.

climate The average weather conditions of a particular place or region over a period of years.

forecast To calculate or guess that something will happen in the future based on data from the past.

hygrometer An instrument for measuring the amount of moisture in the air.

meteorology A science that deals with the atmosphere, weather, and weather forecasting.

observation An act of gathering information by noting facts or occurrences.

precipitation Water that falls to Earth as hail, mist, rain, sleet, or snow.

predictable Able to be foretold.

radar A system that uses waves of energy to sense the location and speed of objects.

riverbed A channel where there is or used to be a river.

spiral Winding or circling around a center.

thermometer An instrument for measuring temperature.

tornado A type of storm in which powerful rotating winds form a column, which reaches toward the ground.

trend A general tendency or movement; a general direction taken.

tropical cyclone A circular storm that forms over warm oceans and brings heavy rains and strong winds; it is also called a hurricane or a typhoon.

vegetation The plant life in an area (trees, grasses, and other plants).

For More Information

Books

Breen, Mark, and Kathleen Friestad. *The Kids' Book of Weather Forecasting*. Milwaukee, WI: Ideals Publishing, 2008.

Cherry, Lynne, and Gary Braasch. *How We Know What We Know About Our Changing Climate: Scientists and Kids Explore Global Warming*. Nevada City, CA: Dawn Publications: 2008.

Mogil, H. Michael. *Extreme Weather*. New York, NY: Simon & Schuster Books for Young Readers, 2011.

Sievert, Terri. *Forecasting Weather*. Mankato, MN: Capstone Press, 2012.

Somervill, Barbara A. *Hurricanes*. North Mankato, MN: Cherry Lake Publishing, 2013.

Websites

Because of the changing nature of Internet links, Rosen Publishing has developed an online list of websites related to the subject of this book. This site is updated regularly. Please use this link to access the list:

http://www.rosenlinks.com/LFO/Fore

Index